The Essence of Kant's

*Groundwork of the
Metaphysics of Morals*

The Essence of Kant's

Groundwork of the Metaphysics of Morals

Edited with an Introduction by
Hunter Lewis

The Essence of . . . series of books are edited versions of great works of moral philosophy, distilled to reveal the essence of their authors' thought and argument. To read the complete, unedited version of this work, and see the excised passages, please visit our website at www.AxiosInstitute.org.

Axios Press
P.O. Box 118
Mount Jackson, VA 22842
888.542.9467   info@axiosinstitute.org

Library of Congress Cataloging-in-Publication Data

    Kant, Immanuel, 1724-1804.
    [Grundlegung zur Metaphysik der Sitten. English]
    The essence of Kant's Groundwork of the metaphysics of morals / edited
    with an Introduction by Hunter Lewis.
    p. cm.
    Some passages have been excised.
    Includes index.
    ISBN 978-1-60419-055-7 (pbk.)
    1. Ethics--Early works to 1800. I. Lewis, Hunter. II. Title.

B2766.E6G7 2012

170--dc23

2012023263

Contents

Introduction

HOW SHOULD WE conduct ourselves in life? And where should we look for guidance? Some of the most celebrated answers have come from the German philosopher Immanuel Kant (1724–1804).

To begin with the second question, we cannot simply rely on teachers, even those who speak with a voice of authority. They will inevitably disagree, and then how to choose? Personal experience is of undoubted use in telling us how to live. Once we learn not to touch a hot stove, we rarely need another lesson. But as we arrive at a fork in an unknown road, experience cannot tell us where to go, and this is equally true in our moral travels.

Kant suggests that our most reliable guide in life is our logical faculty. Look for truths which, subjected to logical tests, never contradict themselves. To be logical, a truth must be clear, complete, relevant, presented in an orderly and organized way, and above all self-consistent. Are there any moral truths that pass these tests?

Kant believes there are, and begins his argument with a first proposition:

> Nothing can possibly be conceived in the world, or even out of it, which can be called good without qualification, except a good will. . . .

> Moderation in the affections and passions, self-control, and calm deliberation are not only good in many respects, but even seem to constitute part of the intrinsic worth of the person. But even these are far from deserving to be called good without qualification, although they have been so unconditionally praised by the ancients. For without the principles of a good will, they may become extremely bad. The coolness of a villain not only makes him far more dangerous, but also directly makes him more abominable in our eyes. . . .

> A good will is good not because of what it performs or achieves, not by its aptness for the attainment of some proposed end, but simply by virtue of what it is. . . .

> We have then to develop the idea of a will which deserves to be highly esteemed for itself and is

good without a view to anything further, an idea which exists already in the sound natural understanding, requiring rather to be cleared up than to be taught. . . . In order to do this, we will take the notion of duty, which includes that of a good will. . . .

It is not always easy to know whether an action reflects a sense of duty or self-interest. . . . It is especially hard to make this distinction when an action accords with duty but the subject has besides a direct inclination to it. For example, it is always a matter of duty that a dealer should not overcharge an inexperienced purchaser, so that a child buys of him like any other. Men are thus honestly served, but this is not enough to make us believe that the tradesman has so acted from duty and from principles of honesty. His own advantage required it [in order not to lose his reputation and thence his customers]. Accordingly the action was done neither from duty nor from direct inclination, but partly from a selfish view. . . .

Similarly, it is a duty to maintain one's life, and, in addition, everyone has a direct inclination to do so. In this case, men preserve their life as duty requires, no doubt, but not because duty requires. . . .

To be beneficent when we can is a duty. And there are many people so sympathetically constituted that, without any other motive of vanity or self-interest, they find pleasure in spreading joy around them and take delight in the satisfaction of others. But I maintain that in such a case an action of this kind, however proper, however amiable it may be, has nevertheless no true moral worth, but is rather on a level with the inclination to honor. . . .

Our second proposition is this: That an action done from duty derives its moral worth, not from what is to be attained by it, but from how it was chosen, and in particular whether the choice was made without reference to personal desire or material ends. . . .

Our third proposition, which follows from the two preceding, I would express thus: Duty is the necessity of acting out of respect for the law. . . . An action done from duty must wholly exclude the influence of inclination and with it every object of the will, so that nothing remains which can determine the will except objectively the law, and subjectively pure respect for this practical law, and consequently the maxim that I should follow this law even to the thwarting of all my inclinations. . . .

But what sort of law is this, which must guide my will, without any regard to the effect expected from it, in order that my will may be called good absolutely and without qualification? It is this: I am never to act otherwise than so that I could will that my maxim should itself become a universal law. This is the general law that serves the will as its principle and must so serve it, if duty is not to be a vain delusion and a chimerical notion. . . .

The shortest way, and an unerring one, to discover whether a lie is consistent with duty, is to ask myself, "Should I be content that my maxim (to extricate myself from difficulty by a false promise) should hold good as a universal law, for myself as well as for others?"; and should I be able to say to myself, "Everyone may make a deceitful promise when he finds himself in a difficulty from which he cannot otherwise extricate himself?"

Then I presently become aware that while I can will the lie, I can by no means will that lying should be a universal law. For with such a law there would be no promises at all, or people would always pay me back in my own coin. Hence my maxim, as soon as it were made a universal law, would necessarily destroy itself.

I do not, therefore, need any far-reaching penetration to discern what I have to do in order that my will may be morally good. Inexperienced in the course of the world, incapable of being prepared for all its contingencies, I only ask myself: Can I will that my maxim should be a universal law? If not, then it must be rejected, not because of a disadvantage accruing from it to myself or even to others, but because it cannot serve as universal legislation, and logic extorts from me immediate respect for such legislation. . . .

Although common men do not conceive this law in such an abstract and universal form, yet they always have it before their eyes and use it as the standard of their decision. . . .

Innocence is indeed a glorious thing; on the other hand, it is easily seduced. On this account even common wisdom, which otherwise consists more in conduct than in knowledge, has need of philosophy, not in order to learn from it, but to secure for its precepts stability and permanence. . . .

We cannot better serve the wishes of those who ridicule all morality as a mere chimera of the human imagination than by conceding to them that notions of duty must be drawn only from experience. To do this is to prepare for those people a certain triumph. . . .

Reason itself, independent of all experience, ordains what ought to take place. Even if there has never been a sincere friend, yet not a whit the less is pure sincerity in friendship required of every man. Prior to all experience, this duty is commanded by reason operating through a priori principles. . . .

The imperative which commands a certain conduct immediately, without having any other purpose to be attained by it, let the consequence be what it may, is categorical. This imperative may also be called that of morality. . . .

There is but one such categorical imperative, namely, this: Act only in such a way as you can will to become a universal law. . . .

This can also be expressed in this form: Act as if the maxim of your action were to become by your will a universal law of nature. . . .

If, then, there is a supreme practical principle that, with respect to the human will, takes the form of a categorical imperative, it must be one that is an end for everyone because it is an *end in itself.* As it constitutes an objective principle, it can serve as a universal practical law. The foundation of this principle is this: rationality is an end for all rational beings because it is an *end in itself*. Every other rational being stands on this same rational ground that holds for me. From this we derive the practical imperative: *So act that you treat humanity, whether in your own person or that of any other, in every case as an end, never only as a means....*

We can now end where we started at the beginning, namely, with the conception of a will unconditionally good. That will is absolutely good which cannot be evil, in other words, whose maxim, if made a universal law, could never contradict itself. This principle, then, is its supreme law: "Act always on such a maxim as you can at the same time will to be a universal law." This is the sole condition under which a will can never contradict itself; such an imperative is categorical. Since the validity of the will as a universal law for possible actions is analogous to the universal connection of the existence of things by general laws, the categorical imperative can also be expressed thus: Act on maxims which can at the same time have for their object themselves as universal laws of nature. Such then is the formula of an absolutely good will. These different ways of expressing the law are just that—they really express the same law. Each implies the other....

Kant's Categorical Imperative is sometimes confused with the Golden Rule. This Rule, which appears in some form in most established world religions, may be expressed as: "Do unto others as you would have them do unto you."* Although there is some similarity with the Categorical Imperative, logicians are correct that there are fundamental differences. An example that has been cited is the case of a masochist. Since he enjoys pain, he might under the Golden Rule argue that it would be right to inflict pain on others.

The preceding example is not meant to denigrate the Golden Rule. It is an extremely important moral concept, one which states emphatically that unrestrained egoism is not an acceptable way of life; that we must live with others; that we must try to be fair to others; and that disregarding this principle will likely lead to results that even the most ardent egoist will not enjoy. The Categorical Imperative further improves on the Golden Rule by offering the universalizability principle which sado-masochism would clearly fail.

Kant argues that the universalizability principle can and must be applied without any regard for empirical circumstances. It is not clear that this is correct. It is clearly correct to argue that universalizing murder would be illogical because it would lead to a world in which no one is left to murder. But let's take a less

---

* Christian Bible, Luke 6:13.

extreme example. What if I ask myself whether it is morally acceptable to live in a mansion? Under today's circumstances, it would not be possible for every human being to live in a mansion: it would require unavailable resources and probably also take up too much of earth's limited space. Under other circumstances, however, such as reduced population or technological advances, perhaps every human being could live in a mansion. Indeed, what is a mansion? The average modern American home would strike most people living today and almost everyone who lived in the past as a mansion.

It may also be argued that universalizability is not quite as clear and complete a concept as Kant thought. When a parent willingly sacrifices his or her life for a child, that is clearly universalizable. It is not an idea that contradicts itself. Moreover, it has further elements of rationality when considered from the point of view of circumstances: the child by definition in all probability has more future years ahead, if its life is preserved, than the parent has to lose.

Let's imagine, however, that you are hiking in the mountains and see a stranger about to fall from a ledge. To rescue the stranger will entail great risk to one's own life. It is not clear that the Categorical Imperative will tell us in this instance what to do.

These caveats aside, the Categorical Imperative is an immense achievement. Its emphasis on intentions over consequences is often contrasted with Jeremy Bentham's *Utilitarianism*, which put the whole emphasis on consequences. *Utilitarianism* leads to odd and unsatisfactory hypothetical choices. Assume, for example, that by killing one innocent person you could save the lives of ten other people. Would you do it? Most mature, moral people would not make this choice. They would feel, and feel strongly, that it is never right to take an innocent life, no matter what the circumstances. Kant reminds us that this principle is logical, and that the competing utilitarian logic can only take us so far before being consumed in self-contradiction.

Life

Immanuel Kant was born in 1724 in Königsberg, then part of Prussia, now in Russia. He remained in the same city his entire life, never married, devoted himself to philosophy, was appointed Professor of Logic and Metaphysics at the University of Königsberg, and wrote innumerable books including the *Critique of Pure Reason* (1781), which became the single most celebrated book in the history of European philosophy; the *Groundwork of the Metaphysics of Morals* (1785), one of the most celebrated works of moral philosophy; the *Critique of Practical Reason* (1788), which expanded on the *Groundwork*; and the *Critique of Judgment* (1790). The only ripple in what otherwise seemed an outwardly uneventful but prodigiously productive career occurred in 1794 when King Friedrich Wilhelm II officially censured Kant for allegedly veering too far from orthodox Christianity in his book of the same year, *Religion within the Limits of Reason Alone*.

Throughout his life and thereafter, Kant was celebrated for his powers of intense concentration on philosophical questions, devotion to routine, and disregard for the outside world. Will Durant recounts how neighbors could set their clocks by Kant's daily walk outside his home, which took place punctually at the same time each afternoon. One day he was allegedly so wrapped up in thought that he forgot to put on a second shoe and thus walked with only one. Whether true or not, the story captures the spirit of one of the most brilliant "absent-minded" geniuses of world history.

—HUNTER LEWIS

Preface

PHYSICS HAS AN empirical and also a rational part. It is the same with Ethics; but here the empirical part might also be called practical anthropology, the rational part also be called morals. . . .

Is it not of the utmost necessity to construct a pure moral philosophy which is not just empirical or belonging to anthropology? That such a philosophy is possible should be evident from the common idea of duty and of the moral laws. Everyone must admit that if a law is to have moral force, i.e., to be the basis of an obligation, it must carry with it absolute necessity; that, for example, the precept, "Thou shalt not lie," is not valid for men alone; other rational beings must also observe it; and so it is with all the other moral laws properly so called. Therefore, the basis of obligation must not be sought in the nature of man, or in the circumstances in the world in which he is placed, but a priori in the conception of pure reason; and although any other precept which is founded on principles of mere experience may be in certain respects universal, yet in so far as it rests even in the least degree on an empirical basis, perhaps only as to a motive, such a precept, while it may be a practical rule, can never be called a moral law.

Moral laws along with their principles are essentially distinguished from every other kind of practical knowledge in which there is anything empirical. All moral philosophy rests wholly on nonempirical ground. When applied to man, it does not borrow anything from the knowledge of man himself (anthropology), but bestows laws a priori to him as a rational being. No doubt these laws require a judgment sharpened by experience, in order to distinguish in what cases they are applicable, and also to help him find the will to make them concrete in his life. . . .

In order that an action should be morally good, it is not enough that it conform to the moral law. It must also be done for the sake of the law; otherwise conformity is only contingent and uncertain. A principle which is not moral may now and then produce actions conformable to the law, but also actions which contradict it. We must, therefore, begin with pure philosophy; without it there cannot be any moral philosophy at all. That which mingles these pure principles with the empirical does not deserve the name of philosophy. . . .

The present treatise is, therefore, nothing more than the investigation and establishment of the supreme principle of morality. This constitutes a study distinct and complete in itself which ought to be kept apart from every other moral investigation. This weighty question has hitherto been very unsatisfactorily examined. . . .

Section I

Transition to a Philosophy of Morals

NOTHING CAN POSSIBLY be conceived in the world, or even out of it, which can be called good without qualification, except a good will. Intelligence, wit, judgment, and the other talents of the mind, along with courage, resolution, perseverance, qualities of temperament, are undoubtedly good and desirable in many respects. But these gifts of nature may also become bad and mischievous if the will which makes use of them, and which, therefore, constitutes what is called character, is not good. It is the same with the gifts of fortune. Power, riches, honor, health, even the general well-being and contentment with one's condition which is called happiness, inspire pride, and often presumption, if there is not a good will to correct the influence of these on the mind, and to govern the whole principle of acting. The sight of a being devoid of a single feature of a pure and good will, but enjoying unbroken prosperity, can never give pleasure to an impartial rational spectator. In order to be worthy of happiness, we must have a good will. . . .

Moderation in the affections and passions, self-control, and calm deliberation are not only good in many respects, but even seem to constitute part of the intrinsic worth of the person. But even these are far from deserving to be called good without qualification, although they have been so unconditionally praised by the ancients. For without the principles of a good will, they may become extremely bad. The coolness of a villain not only makes him far more dangerous, but also directly makes him more abominable in our eyes. . . .

A good will is good not because of what it performs or achieves, not by its aptness for the attainment of some proposed end, but simply by virtue of what it is. It is good in itself. Even if it should happen that, owing to a special disfavor of fortune, or a poor provision of nature, this will should wholly lack power to accomplish its purpose, even if with its greatest efforts it should yet achieve nothing, and there should remain only the good will, then, like a jewel, it would still shine by its own light, as a thing which has its whole value in itself. Its usefulness or fruitlessness can neither add nor take away anything from this value. . . .

There is, however, something strange in this idea of the absolute value of a good will, in which no account is taken of its utility. Notwithstanding the thorough assent of common reason to the idea, a suspicion may arise that it is the product of mere high-flown fancy, and that we may have misunderstood. Therefore we will examine this idea further. . . .

In a being with reason and a will, if the proper object of nature is its conservation, its welfare, in a word, its happiness, then nature would have hit upon a very bad arrangement in relying on the reason of the creature. For all the actions which the creature has to perform in order to achieve this happiness, and the whole rule of its conduct, would be far more surely prescribed to it by instinct. . . .

In fact, we find that the more a cultivated reason applies itself with deliberate purpose to the enjoyment of life and happiness, the more the man fails of true satisfaction. And from this circumstance there arises in many, if they are candid, some degree of hatred for reason, because after calculating all the advantages derived, not only from the invention of all the arts of common luxury, but even from the sciences they find that they have, in fact, only brought more trouble on their shoulders, not happiness. And they end by envying, rather than despising, the more common stamp of men who keep closer to the guidance of mere instinct and do not allow their reason much influence on their conduct. . . . From these judgments another idea emerges: that our existence has a different and far nobler end than happiness, to which reason will lead us, and which will require that we put aside our more common purposes.

For as reason is not competent to guide the will with certainty in regard to the satisfaction of all our wants (which to some extent it even multiplies), the real purpose of reason must be to produce a will, not merely good as a means to something else, but good in itself, for which purpose reason is absolutely necessary. . . . If then reason in many ways may interfere, at least in this life, with happiness, then nature has not failed of its purpose, because the establishment of a good will is its purpose. . . .

We have then to develop the idea of a will which deserves to be highly esteemed for itself and is good without a view to anything further, an idea which exists already in the sound natural understanding, requiring rather to be cleared up than to be taught, and which in estimating the value of our actions always takes the first place and constitutes the condition of all the rest. In order to do this, we will take the notion of duty, which includes that of a good will, although implying certain subjective restrictions and hindrances. These, however, far from concealing it, or rendering it unrecognizable, rather make it shine the brighter. . . .

It is not always easy to know whether an action reflects a sense of duty or self-interest. . . . It is especially hard to make this distinction when an action accords with duty but the subject has besides a direct inclination to it. For example, it is always a matter of duty that a dealer should not overcharge an inexperienced purchaser, so that a child buys of him like any other. Men are thus honestly served, but this is not enough to make us believe that the tradesman has so acted from duty and from principles of honesty. His own advantage required it [in order not to lose his reputation and thence his customers]. Accordingly the action was done neither from duty nor from direct inclination, but partly from a selfish view. . . .

Similarly, it is a duty to maintain one's life, and, in addition, everyone has a direct inclination to do so. In this case, men preserve their life as duty requires, no doubt, but not because duty requires. . . .

To be beneficent when we can is a duty. And there are many people so sympathetically constituted that, without any other motive of vanity or self-interest, they find pleasure in spreading joy around them and take delight in the satisfaction of others. But I maintain that in such a case an action of this kind, however proper, however amiable it may be, has nevertheless no true moral worth, but is rather on a level with the inclination to honor. If it is happily directed to that which is in fact of public utility and accordant with duty, it deserves praise and encouragement, but not esteem.

For the action lacks the moral criterion, namely, that it be done from duty, not from inclination. . . .

To secure one's own happiness is a duty, at least indirectly. For discontent with one's condition, under a pressure of many anxieties and amidst unsatisfied wants, might easily become a great temptation to a transgression of duty. But here again, all men already have the strongest and most intimate inclination to happiness, although it may be pursued confusedly. A gouty patient, for instance, may choose to enjoy what he likes, and to suffer what he may, since, according to his calculation, on this occasion at least, he has not sacrificed the enjoyment of the present moment to a possibly mistaken expectation of a happiness which is supposed to be found in health. . . . But here, as in all other cases, he should promote his happiness, not from inclination but from duty, and only in this way would his conduct acquire true moral worth. . . .

Our second proposition is this: That an action done from duty derives its moral worth, not from what is to be attained by it, but from how it was chosen, and in particular whether the choice was made without reference to personal desire or material ends. . . .

Our third proposition, which follows from the two preceding, I would express thus: Duty is the necessity of acting out of respect for the law. . . . An action done from duty must wholly exclude the influence of inclination and with it every object of the will, so that nothing remains which can determine the will except objectively the law, and subjectively pure respect for this practical law, and consequently the maxim that I should follow this law even to the thwarting of all my inclinations. . . .

But what sort of law is this, which must guide my will, without any regard to the effect expected from it, in order that my will may be called good absolutely and without qualification? It is this: I am never to act otherwise than so that I could will that my maxim should itself become a universal law. This is the general law that serves the will as its principle and must so serve it, if duty is not to be a vain delusion and a chimerical notion. The common reason of men in practical judgments perfectly coincides with this and always has in view the principle here suggested.

For example: May I in distress make a promise with the intention not to keep it? I readily distinguish here between whether it is prudent and whether it is right to make a false promise. I may see clearly that it is not enough to extricate myself from a present difficulty by means of this subterfuge, that it must also be well considered whether there may not hereafter spring from this lie much greater inconvenience than that from which I now free myself, and that with all my supposed cunning, the consequences cannot be so easily foreseen. But it is soon clear to me that such a maxim will still only be based on the fear of consequences.

It is a wholly different thing to be truthful from duty. The shortest way, and an unerring one, to discover whether a lie is consistent with duty, is to ask myself, "Should I be content that my maxim (to extricate myself from difficulty by a false promise) should hold good as a universal law, for myself as well as for others?"; and should I be able to say to myself, "Everyone may make a deceitful promise when he finds himself in a difficulty from which he cannot otherwise extricate himself"?

Then I presently become aware that while I can will the lie, I can by no means will that lying should be a universal law. For with such a law there would be no promises at all, or people would always pay me back in my own coin. Hence my maxim, as soon as it were made a universal law, would necessarily destroy itself.

I do not, therefore, need any far-reaching penetration to discern what I have to do in order that my will may be morally good. Inexperienced in the course of the world, incapable of being prepared for all its contingencies, I only ask myself: Can I will that thy maxim should be a universal law? If not, then it must be rejected, not because of a disadvantage accruing from it to myself or even to others, but because it cannot serve as universal legislation, and reason extorts from me immediate respect for such legislation. I do not indeed as yet discern on what this respect is based (about this the philosopher may inquire), but at least I grasp the principle that a will which is good in itself is above everything. . . .

Although common men do not conceive this law in such an abstract and universal form, yet they always have it before their eyes and use it as the standard of their decision. It would be easy to show how, with this compass in hand, men are well able to distinguish, in every case that occurs, what is good, what bad, conformable to duty or inconsistent with it. We do not need science and philosophy to know what we should do to be honest and good, yea, even wise and virtuous. . . .

Here we can only express admiration when we see how great an advantage the practical judgment has over the theoretical in the common understanding of men. If common reason ventures to depart from the laws of experience and from the perceptions of the senses, it falls into mere inconceivabilities and self-contradictions, at least into a chaos of uncertainty, obscurity, and instability. But in the practical sphere, it begins to show itself to advantage. . . .

It may even have as good a hope of hitting the mark as any philosopher. Nay, it is almost more sure of doing so, because the philosopher may easily perplex his judgment by a multitude of considerations foreign to the matter, and so turn aside from the right way. Would it not therefore be wiser in moral concerns to acquiesce in the judgment of common reason, or at most only to call in philosophy for the purpose of rendering the system of morals more complete and intelligible, and its rules more convenient for use? . . .

Innocence is indeed a glorious thing; on the other hand, it is easily seduced. On this account even common wisdom, which otherwise consists more in conduct than in knowledge, has need of philosophy, not in order to learn from it, but to secure for its precepts stability and permanence. Against the commands of duty (which common reason represents as so deserving of respect), each man also feels in himself a powerful counterpoise in his wants and inclinations, the entire satisfaction of which he sums up under the name of happiness. Reason issues its commands unyieldingly, without promising anything to the inclinations, and, as it were, with disregard and contempt for these claims, which are so impetuous, and at the same time so plausible. Hence there arises a natural dialectic, a disposition to argue against these strict laws of duty, to question their validity, or at least their purity and strictness, and, if possible, to make them more accordant with our wishes and inclinations, that is, to corrupt them at their very source and entirely to destroy their worth. . . .

Thus is the common reason of man compelled to go out of its sphere, and to take a step into the field of philosophy, so that it may escape from the perplexity of opposite claims and not run the risk of losing all genuine moral principles through equivocation.

When practical reason cultivates itself, there insensibly arises in it a process which forces it to seek aid in philosophy. It will not otherwise find rest but in a thorough critical examination of our reason.

Section II

Transition from Popular Morals to a Philosophy of Morals

IF WE HAVE hitherto drawn our notion of duty from the common use of our practical reason, it is by no means to be inferred that we have treated it as an empirical notion. On the contrary, if we examine the experience of men's conduct, we meet frequent and just complaints that one cannot find a single certain example of the disposition to act from pure duty. Although many things are done in conformity with what duty prescribes, it is always doubtful whether they are done strictly from duty, so as to have a moral worth.

Hence there have at all times been philosophers who have altogether denied that this disposition actually exists in human actions, and have ascribed everything to a more or less refined self-love. Not that they have for that reason questioned the soundness of the conception of morality; on the contrary, they spoke with sincere regret of the frailty and corruption of human nature, which, though noble enough to take as its rule an idea so worthy of respect, is yet too weak to follow it. . . .

It is absolutely impossible to make out from experience with complete certainty a single case in which indeed an action, however right in itself, was undertaken solely on moral grounds and on the concept of duty. Sometimes it happens that with the sharpest self-examination we can find nothing beside the moral principle of duty which could have been powerful enough to move us to this or that action and to so great a sacrifice. But even then we cannot infer with certainty that it was not really some secret impulse of self-love, under the false appearance of duty, that was the actual determining cause of the will.

We like to flatter ourselves by falsely taking credit for a more noble motive, whereas in fact we can never, even by the strictest examination, get completely behind the secret springs of action. When the question is of moral worth, it is not with the visible actions that we are concerned, but with the inward principles behind them which we do not see.

We cannot better serve the wishes of those who ridicule all morality as a mere chimera of the human imagination than by conceding to them that notions of duty must be drawn only from experience. To do this is to prepare for those people a certain triumph. I am willing to admit out of love of humanity that most of our actions are correct, but if we look closer at them we everywhere come upon the dear self which is always prominent, not the strict command of duty which often requires self-denial. Without being an enemy of virtue, a cool observer, may sometimes doubt whether true virtue is actually found anywhere in the world, especially so as years advance and the judgment is made wiser by experience and more acute in observation.

This being so, nothing can secure us from falling away altogether from our ideas of duty, and our respect for its law, but the clear conviction that whether this or that takes place is not at all the question. Reason itself, independent of all experience, ordains what ought to take place. Even if there has never been a sincere friend, yet not a whit the less is pure sincerity in friendship required of every man. Prior to all experience, this duty is commanded by reason operating through a priori principles. . . .

For a law to be valid, it must apply not merely to men but to all rational creatures generally, not merely under certain contingent conditions or with exceptions but with absolute necessity. It should be clear that no experience will enable us to infer even the possibility of such laws, especially under the contingent conditions of humanity. . . .

Nor could anything be more fatal to morality than that we should wish to derive it from examples. Every example that is set before us must first be tested by principles of morality, to see whether it is worthy to serve as an example, i.e., as a pattern. Even the Holy One of the Gospels must first be compared with our ideal of moral perfection before we can recognize Him as such. So He says of Himself, "Why call you Me (whom you see) good; none is good (the model of good) but God only (whom you do not see)?"

And from whence have we the conception of God as the supreme good? Simply from the idea of moral perfection, which reason frames a priori and connects inseparably with the notion of a free will. Imitation finds no place at all in morality; examples serve only for encouragement, i.e., they render beyond doubt the feasibility of what the law commands, they make visible that which the practical rule expresses more abstractly, but it will never suffice to guide ourselves by examples. . . .

This descending to popular notions is certainly commendable, if the ascent to the principles of pure reason has first been satisfactorily accomplished. This implies that we first found ethics on reason, and then, when it is firmly established, procure a hearing for it by giving it a popular character. It is quite absurd to try to be popular in the first step, on which the later steps follow. To do so just produces a disgusting medley of compiled observations and half-reasoned principles. Shallow minds may enjoy this, because it can be used for everyday conversation, but the wise find in it only confusion, and if philosophers, see quite well through this delusion. . . .

Moralists who operate in this fashion offer as our underpinning or our goal at one point some perfection, at another happiness, here moral sense, there fear of God, a little of this, and a little of that, in marvelous mixture, without it occurring to them to ask whether the principles of morality are to be found at all in human nature or empirical experience, as opposed to pure reason, from which practical rules then be deduced. . . .

Such a philosophy of morals, completely isolated, not mixed with any anthropology, theology, or physics, and still less with the occult, is indispensable. It exercises on the human heart, through reason alone, an influence so much more powerful than all other forces derived from experience. . . .

I have a letter from the late excellent Sulzer, in which he asks me what can be the reason that moral instruction, although containing much that is convincing for the reason, yet accomplishes so little? My answer is simply this: that the teachers themselves have not got their own notions clear, and when they endeavor to make up for this by raking together motives of moral goodness from every quarter, trying to make their medicine right strong, they spoil it. For the commonest understanding shows that if we imagine, on the one hand, an act of honesty done with steadfast mind, apart from every view to advantage of any kind in this world or another, and even under the greatest temptations of necessity or allurement, and, on the other hand, a similar act which was affected, in however low a degree, by a foreign motive, the former leaves far behind and eclipses the second; it elevates the soul and inspires the wish to be able to act in like manner oneself. Even moderately young children feel this impression, and one should never represent duties to them in any other light. . . .

From what has been said, it is clear that all moral conceptions have their seat and origin completely a priori in the reason, and that, moreover, in the commonest reason just as truly as in that which is in the highest degree speculative; that they cannot be obtained from any empirical, and therefore merely contingent, knowledge; that it is just this purity of their origin that makes them worthy to serve as our supreme practical principle; and that it is of the greatest practical importance, to derive these notions and laws from pure reason, to present them pure and unmixed. In short, since moral laws ought to hold good for every rational creature, we must derive them from the general concept of a rational being. . . .

In order to advance further by natural steps, we must follow and clearly describe the practical faculty of reason, from the general rules of its determination to the point where the notion of duty springs from it. . . .

An objective principle, in so far as it obligates our will, is called a command (of reason), and the formula of the command is called an imperative. . . .

No imperatives hold for the Divine will, or in general for a holy will. Ought is here out of place, because the volition is already of itself necessarily in unison with the law. But they do apply to the imperfect will of a rational being, e.g., the human will.

Now all imperatives command either hypothetically or categorically. The former represent the practical necessity of an action as a means to something else that is willed. The categorical imperative by contrast represents an action which is objectively necessary without reference to a further end. If the action is good only as a means to something else, then the imperative is hypothetical; if it is good in itself and necessary in order to conform to reason, then it is categorical. . . .

The choice of means to our own greatest well-being may be called prudence. The word prudence is used in two ways: the first involves a man's ability to influence others so as to use them for his own purposes. The second involves the sagacity to combine all purposes for his own lasting benefit. When a man is prudent in the former sense, but not in the latter, we might better say of him that he is clever and cunning, but, on the whole, imprudent. But even with this distinction, the imperative which governs the choice of means to one's own happiness, i.e., the precept of prudence, is still always hypothetical. The action is not commanded absolutely, but only as means to another purpose.

The imperative which commands a certain conduct immediately, without having any other purpose to be attained by it, let the consequence be what it may, is categorical. This imperative may also be called that of morality. . . .

No special explanation is needed to show how an imperative of skill is possible. If I know that it is only by a process that an intended operation can be performed, then, if I fully will the operation, I also will the action required for it. It is one and the same thing to conceive something as an effect which I can produce in a certain way, and to conceive myself as acting in this way. . . .

If it were equally easy to give a definite concept of happiness, the imperatives of prudence would be similar to those of skill, and equally analytical. For in this case as in that, it could be said: "Whoever wills the end wills also (according to the necessary dictate of reason) the indispensable means which are in his power." Unfortunately, however, the notion of happiness is so uncertain that although every man wishes to attain it, yet he never can say definitely and consistently what it is that he really wishes and wills. . . .

It is impossible that even the most clear-sighted being should frame to himself a definite conception of what he really wills in this. Does he will riches? How much anxiety, envy, and snares might he not thereby draw upon his shoulders? Does he will knowledge and discernment? It might prove to be only an eye so much the sharper to show him the evils that are now concealed from him, that cannot be avoided, or to impose more wants on his desires, which already give him concern enough. Would he have long life? Who guarantees to him that it would not be a long misery? Would he at least have health? How often has uneasiness of the body restrained us from excesses into which perfect health would have allowed us to fall? And so on. In short, he is unable, on any principle, to determine with certainty what would make him truly happy; because to do so he would need to be omniscient.

We cannot therefore act on any definite principles to secure happiness, but only on empirical guide rules, e.g., of regimen, frugality, courtesy, reserve, etc., which experience recommends on the average, to promote well-being. It follows from this that imperatives of prudence do not, strictly speaking, command us at all; they are rather to be regarded as counsels, not precepts of reason. . . .

We shall have to investigate a priori (via pure logic) the possibility of a categorical imperative, since we cannot derive it from experience. Only this categorical imperative has the standing of a practical law; all the rest may indeed be principles of the will but not laws, since whatever is only necessary for the attainment of some arbitrary purpose may be considered as in itself contingent, and we can at any time be free from the principle if we give up the purpose. By contrast, an unconditional command leaves the will no liberty to choose the opposite; consequently it alone may be described as a law. . . .

There is but one such categorical imperative, namely, this: Act only in such a way as you can will to become a universal law. . . .

This can also be expressed in this form: Act as if the maxim of your action were to become by your will a universal law of nature.

We will now enumerate a few duties, adopting the usual division of them into duties to ourselves and both to ourselves and to others, and into those which brook no exception and those where the duty is somewhat less strict. . . .

1. A man reduced to despair by a series of misfortunes feels wearied of life, but is still so far in possession of his reason that he can ask himself whether it would not be contrary to his duty to himself to take his

own life. He inquires whether the maxim of his action could become a universal law of nature. His maxim is: "From self-love, I adopt it as a principle to shorten my life when its longer duration is likely to bring more evil than satisfaction." Can this principle founded on self-love become a universal law of nature? We see at once that a system of nature of which it should be a law to destroy life would contradict itself and, therefore, could not exist as a system of nature. This maxim cannot possibly exist as a universal law of nature and, consequently, would be inconsistent with the categorical imperative.

2. Another finds himself forced by necessity to borrow money. He knows that he will not be able to repay it, but sees also that nothing will be lent to him unless he promises stoutly to repay it in a definite time. He desires to make this promise, but he has enough conscience to ask himself: "Is it not unlawful and inconsistent with duty to get out of a difficulty in this way?" Suppose however that he resolves to do so anyway: then the maxim of his action would be expressed thus: "When I think myself in want of money, I will borrow money and

promise to repay it, although I know that I never can do so. . . . Is this right?" I convert the suggestion of self-love into a universal law, and state the question thus: "How would it be if my maxim were a universal law?" Then I see at once that it could never hold as a universal law of nature, but would necessarily contradict itself. For supposing it to be a universal law that everyone when he thinks himself in a difficulty should be able to promise whatever he pleases, with the purpose of not keeping his promise, the promise itself would become useless, the end that one might have in view unattainable. No one would pay attention to anything promised him, but would ridicule all such statements as vain pretences.

3. A third finds in himself a talent which with cultivation might make him a useful man in many respects. But he prefers to indulge in pleasure. He asks, however, whether his way of life agrees with what is called duty. He sees that some men (like the South Sea islanders) let their talents lie unused and devote their lives merely to idleness, amusement, and propagation of their species—in a word, to enjoyment. But he cannot possibly will that this should be a universal law

of nature, or be implanted in us by a natural instinct. For, as a rational being, he necessarily wills that his faculties be developed, since they serve him and have been given him, for all sorts of possible purposes.

4. A fourth, who is prosperous, sees that others have to contend with great wretchedness and that he could help them. He may think: "What concern is it of mine? Let everyone be as happy as Heaven pleases, or as he can make himself; I will take nothing from him nor contribute anything to his welfare or to his assistance in distress!" If such a mode of thinking were a universal law, the human race might very well subsist and doubtless would be better off than if everyone talks of sympathy and good will, or even takes care occasionally to put it into practice, but also cheats when he can, betrays the rights of men, or otherwise violates them. But it is impossible to will that such a principle should have the universal validity of a law of nature. A will which resolved thus would contradict itself, inasmuch as many instances might occur in which one would need the love and sympathy of others, but in which, by such a law of nature, there would be no hope of aid. . . .

Some actions are of such a character that their maxim cannot without contradiction even be conceived as a universal law of nature. Others do not exhibit this immediate and intrinsic impossibility but it is nevertheless impossible on reflection to will that their maxim should be raised to the universality of a law of nature, since such a will would contradict itself. The former actions violate what we have earlier called strict or inflexible duty; the latter may be subject to a less strict duty. . . .

If now we observe ourselves when transgressing of duty, we find that we do not will that our maxim should be a universal law, for that is impossible for us. On the contrary, we will that the opposite should remain a universal law, but that we may assume the liberty of making an exception in our own favor or just for this time only in favor of our inclination. If we considered all cases from one and the same point of view, namely, that of reason, we should find a contradiction in our own will, namely, that a certain principle objectively should be a universal law, and yet from our subjective point of view should not be universal, but admit of exceptions in our favor. . . .

There is not really any contradiction here, but an antagonism of inclination toward the precept of reason, designed to change the universality of the principle into a mere generality, so that it will meet us half way. Although this cannot be justified according to an impartial judgment, yet it proves that we do really recognize the validity of the categorical imperative. We just want to allow ourselves a few exceptions, which we think unimportant or forced from us.

We have now established at least this much, that if duty is an idea which is to have any real legislative authority over our actions, it can only be expressed in categorical and not in hypothetical terms. We have also exhibited clearly and definitely for every practical application the content of the categorical imperative, which must contain the principle of all duty if such a thing exists. We have not yet, however, advanced so far as to prove a priori that there actually is such an imperative, that there is a practical law commanding absolutely of itself, not from any other impulse, and that to follow this law is our duty. . . .

This leads to the following question: "Is it a necessary law for all rational beings to judge their own actions relying on maxims which they themselves will to be universal laws?" If this law exists, it must be connected (a priori) with the very concept of the will of a rational being. In order to discover this connection we must, however reluctantly, take a step into metaphysics, although into a domain of it which is distinct from speculative philosophy, namely, the metaphysics of morals. If morals were empirical, we would speak of an empirical psychology, which would be part of physics. But as noted before we are concerned here with the relation of the will to itself as determined by reason alone, which excludes anything empirical, a reason which is only found in rational beings. . . .

If, then, there is a supreme practical principle that, with respect to the human will, takes the form of a categorical imperative, it must be one that is an end for everyone because it is an *end in itself*. As it constitutes an objective principle, it can serve as a universal practical law. The foundation of this principle is this: rationality is an end for all rational beings because it is an *end in itself*. Every other rational being stands on this same rational ground that holds for me. From this we derive the practical imperative: *So act that you treat humanity, whether in your own person or that of any other, in every case as an end, never only as a means.* We shall now inquire whether this can be practically carried out.

To return to the previous examples:

■ First: Anyone who contemplates suicide should ask himself whether his action is consistent with the idea of humanity as an end in itself. If he destroys himself in order to escape from painful circumstances, he is using a person merely as a means to maintain a tolerable condition up to the end of life. But a man is not a thing, something that can be used merely as means. I cannot, therefore, dispose in any way of a man (in my own person), mutilate him, damage, or kill him. There is more to say of this, but that discussion belongs to morals, not to the metaphysics of morals, e.g., that it is permitted to amputate a limb in order to save a life, or to undergo danger in order to preserve life. . . .

■ Second: As regards necessary duties towards others, he who is thinking of making a false promise to others will see at once that he would be using others merely as a means. This violation of the principle of humanity in other men is more obvious if we take as our examples attacks on the freedom and property of others. For then it is clear that he who transgresses the rights of men intends to use the person of others merely as a means, without considering that as rational beings they ought always to be esteemed also as ends. In considering this, we should avoid the error of thinking that the common "*quod tibi non vis fieri*, etc." ["Do not do to others what you would not wish them to do to you"] is equivalent to a categorical imperative. It is merely a further deduction, but with several limitations. It cannot be a universal law, for it does not contain the principle of duties to oneself, nor of the duties of benevolence to others (for many a one would gladly consent that others should not benefit him, provided only that he might be excused from showing benevolence to them), nor finally that of duties of strict obligation to one another, for on this principle the criminal might argue against the judge who punishes him, and so on. . . .

■ Third: As regards contingent (not so strict) duties to oneself, it is not sufficient that our action does not violate humanity in our own person, regarding ourselves as an end in itself. It must also harmonize with our being an end in itself. There are in humanity capacities of achieving greater perfection. To neglect these might perhaps be consistent with the maintenance of humanity, but not with the view of humanity as an end rather than a means.

■ Fourth: As regards less strict duties towards others, the humanity might indeed survive, without anyone contributing anything to the happiness of others. But the end of any person who is an end in himself ought as far as possible to be my end also. . . .

From this principle, that humanity, and in general every rational nature, is *an end in itself* . . . there follows the idea that *the will of every rational being is a universal lawgiver.*

On this principle all maxims are rejected which are inconsistent with the will itself being a universal legislator. Thus the will is not simply subject to the law, but must also be regarded as itself giving the law. . . .

Looking back now on all previous attempts to discover the principle of morality, we need not wonder why they all failed. It was recognized that man was bound to laws by duty, but it was not observed that the laws to which he is subject are those of his own giving, though at the same time universal, and that he is only bound to act in conformity with his own will, a will designed by nature to give universal laws. I will call this the principle of autonomy of the will, in contrast with every other which I accordingly reckon as heteronomy.

The conception of the will of every rational being as one which makes and is subject to all the universal laws leads to another, namely, the kingdom of ends.

By a kingdom I understand the union of different rational beings in a system of common laws. A rational being belongs as a member to the kingdom of ends when, although giving universal laws in it, he is also himself subject to these laws. He belongs to it as sovereign when, while giving laws, he is not subject to the will of any other. . . .

Morality consists then in the conformance of action to the legislation which alone can render a kingdom of ends possible. This legislation must be capable of existing in every rational being and of emanating from his will, so that this will cannot act on any maxim which could not without contradiction be a universal law and, accordingly, be chosen by that will. If the maxims of rational beings are not by their own nature coincident with this objective principle, then the necessity of acting on it is called duty. Duty does not apply to the sovereign in the kingdom of ends, but it does to every member of it and to all in the same degree.

The practical necessity of acting on this principle, i.e., duty, does not rest at all on feelings, impulses, or inclinations, but solely on the relation of rational beings to one another, a relation in which the will of a rational being must always be regarded as legislative, since otherwise it could not be conceived as an end in itself. Reason then refers every maxim of the will, regarding it as legislating universally, to every other will and also to every action towards itself; and this not on account of any other practical motive or any future advantage, but from the idea of the dignity of a rational being, obeying no law but that which he himself also gives. . . .

Morality is the condition under which alone a rational being can be an end in himself, since by this alone is it possible that he should be a legislating member in the kingdom of ends. Morality, and humanity as capable of it, is that which alone has dignity. Skill and diligence in labor have a market value;

wit, lively imagination, and humor, have a rare value. On the other hand, fidelity to promises, benevolence from principle (not from instinct), have an intrinsic worth. Neither nature nor art contains anything which in default of these it could put in their place, for their worth consists not in the effects which spring from them, not in the use and advantage which they secure, but in the disposition of mind, that is, the maxims of the will which are ready to manifest themselves in such actions, even though they should not have the desired effect. These actions also need no recommendation from any subjective taste or sentiment, that they may be looked on with immediate favor and satisfaction. They need no immediate propensity or feeling for them; they exhibit the will that performs them as an object of immediate respect, and nothing but reason is required to impose them on the will. It isn't necessary to flatter the will which, in the case of duties, would be a contradiction. These actions are above all value, they define dignity. They have an unconditional and incomparable worth. . . .

We can now end where we started at the beginning, namely, with the conception of a will unconditionally good. That will is absolutely good which cannot be evil, in other words, whose maxim, if made a universal law, could never contradict itself. This principle, then, is its supreme law: "Act always on such a maxim as you can at the same time will to be a universal law." This is the sole condition under which a will can never contradict itself; such an imperative is categorical. Since the validity of the will as a universal law for possible actions is analogous to the universal connection of the existence of things by general laws, the categorical imperative can also be expressed thus: Act on maxims which can at the same time have for their object themselves as universal laws of nature. Such then is the formula of an absolutely good will. These different ways of expressing the law are just that—they really express the same law. Each implies the other. . . .

How such a synthetic practical a priori proposition is possible, and why it is necessary, is a problem whose solution does not lie within the bounds of the metaphysics of morals. We have not here affirmed its truth, much less professed to have a proof of it in our power. We simply showed by the development of the universally received notion of morality that an autonomy of the will is inevitably connected with it, or rather is its foundation. Whoever then holds morality to be anything real, and not a chimerical idea without any truth, must likewise admit the view that is here presented. This section then, like the first, was merely analytical. The next step is to prove that morality is no creation of the brain, which it cannot be if the categorical imperative and with it the autonomy of the will is true, and as an a priori principle absolutely necessary. For this we will need a synthetic use of pure practical reason, which however we cannot venture on without first giving a critical examination of this faculty of reason. We shall proceed to this in the next section. . . .

Section III

Transition from the Metaphysics of Morals to the Critique of Pure Practical Reason

The Concept of Freedom is the Key that Explains the Autonomy of the Will

THE PRECEDING DEFINITION of freedom is negative and therefore unfruitful for the discovery of its essence. But it leads to a positive conception which is more fruitful. The conception of causality involves that of laws, according to which, by something that we call cause, something else, namely the effect, must be produced. Hence, although freedom is not a property of the will depending on physical laws, yet it is not for that reason lawless. On the contrary, it must be a causality acting according to immutable laws, but of a peculiar kind. Otherwise a free will would be an absurdity. What else then can freedom of the will be but autonomy, that is, the property of the will to be a law to itself? But the proposition: "The will is in every action a law to itself," only expresses the principle: "To act on no other maxim than that which can also have as an object itself as a universal law." This is precisely the formula of the categorical imperative and is the principle of morality, so that a free will and a will subject to moral laws are one and the same.

On the hypothesis, then, of freedom of the will, morality together with its principle follows from it by mere analysis of the concept. But some further thought is required. . . .

It must be freely admitted that there is a sort of circle here from which it seems impossible to escape. In the order of efficient causes we assume ourselves free, in order that in the order of ends we may conceive ourselves as subject to moral laws. And we afterwards conceive ourselves as subject to these laws, because we have attributed to ourselves freedom of will. Freedom and self-legislation of will are both autonomy and, therefore, are reciprocal conceptions, and for this very reason one must not be used to explain the other. . . .

One resource remains to us, namely, to inquire whether we do not occupy different points of view when by means of freedom we think ourselves as causes efficient a priori and when we form our conception of ourselves from our actions as effects which we see before our eyes. . . .

As a rational being, belonging to the intelligible world, man can never conceive the causality of his own will otherwise than on condition of the idea of freedom. The idea of freedom is inseparably connected with the conception of autonomy, and this again with the universal principle of morality which is ideally the foundation of all actions of rational beings, just as the law of nature is of all phenomena.

The suspicion raised above is now removed. There is no circle involved in our reasoning from freedom to autonomy, and from this to the moral law. Now we see that, when we conceive ourselves as free, we transfer ourselves into the world of understanding as members of it and recognize the autonomy of the will with its consequence, morality; whereas, if we conceive ourselves as under obligation, we consider ourselves as belonging to the world of sense and at the same time to the world of understanding. . . .

The practical use of common human reason confirms this. There is no one, not even the most consummate villain (provided only that he is otherwise accustomed to the use of reason) who, when we set before him examples of honesty of purpose, of steadfastness in following good maxims, of sympathy and general benevolence, even of great sacrifices of advantages and comfort, does not wish that he might also possess these qualities. Because of his inclinations and impulses, he cannot attain this in himself, but at the same time he wishes to be free from such inclinations which are burdensome to himself. He proves by this that he transfers himself in thought with a will free from the impulses of sensibility into an order of things wholly different from that of his desires. He is conscious of a good will, which by his own confession, constitutes law for the bad will that he possesses as a member of the world of sense—a law whose authority he recognizes while transgressing it. . . .

In order indeed that a rational being who is also affected through the senses should will what reason alone directs, it is no doubt requisite that reason should have a power to infuse a feeling of pleasure or satisfaction in the fulfillment of duty. But it is quite impossible to discern, i.e., to make intelligible a priori, how a mere thought, which itself contains nothing sensible, can itself produce a sensation of pleasure or pain. We can only consult experience about it. But as this cannot supply us with any relation of cause and effect except between two objects of experience, it is quite impossible to explain. . . .

The question of "How a categorical imperative is possible," can be answered to this extent, that we can identify the only hypothesis on which it is possible, namely, the hypothesis of freedom. We can discern the necessity of this hypothesis, and this is sufficient for the practical exercise of reason, that is, for the conviction of the validity of the imperative, and hence of the moral law. But to explain how pure reason can be of itself practical without the aid of any spring of action that could be derived from any other source is beyond the power of human reason, and all the labor and pains of seeking an explanation of it will not avail. . . .

It is no fault of our deduction of the supreme principle of morality, that it does not enable us to conceive the absolute necessity of an unconditional practical law (such as the categorical imperative must be). This is all that can be fairly demanded of a philosophy which strives to carry its principles up to the very limit of human reason.

Index